MW01088611

HAGAR POEMS

HAGAR POEMS

MOHJA KAHF

FOREWORD BY AMINA WADUD

The University of Arkansas Press
Fayetteville
2016

Copyright © 2016 by The University of Arkansas Press
All rights reserved
Manufactured in the United States of America

ISBN: 978-1-68226-000-5
e-ISBN: 978-1-61075-588-7

20 19 18 17 16   5 4 3 2 1

Designed by Liz Lester

⊛ The paper used in this publication meets the minimum requirements
of the American National Standard for Permanence of Paper
for Printed Library Materials Z39.48-1984.

Library of Congress Control Number: 2016933275

To all the Hajars

FOREWORD

This brilliant collection of poems captures all the "patient thread-ing of relationship" between Hagar and Sarah as between women, and then between women and men, between human and God. Yet in the clash of paradox these poems resist the single tightrope of either friend or foe since both—and many more—happen all at the one time. It is hard to resist the single camera lens profil-ing one woman as incomplete in order to highlight the merits in the struggle of the other, but Mohja Kahf synchronizes, cas-cades, climbs, falls, and above all dances to a beat played within an un-rhythmic heartbeat. Herein are women as mothers and caretakers, rebels and fighters, fully frivolous and ripe, riding on a motorcycle. Here they honor each sublime configuration of what exists between them and because of them. There is passion, Kmart, rivers and deserts, and every other unfolding of women before forces that would seek to bind us and keep us small.

In these poems, Kahf lays it all bare, sometimes even to embarrassment—is that not part of what marks us as human and women? At every turn of the page she refuses complacency and circumstance but opts instead for exposing the tenuousness of threads that tie and bind and then come loose before our eyes. The women in these poems can birth a nation and then come back to destroy it. With that destruction we are all invited to destroy our tendency to rely upon a single narrative in what truly matters in life stories. Not only does she take on patriarchy in all its guises, she avoids the bland attempts to then make women out to be perfect. Even God is not relegated to a single uncondi-tional ideal, secure upon a shiny throne. After all, how do we face betrayal from all we hold sacred, dear, handy, and inconvenient, without then betraying ourselves? How do we love, and defy the assault of, a friend who is an "inextractable thorn" in the flesh? We, read, then read again and ponder.

—Dr. Amina Wadud

ACKNOWLEDGMENTS

I am grateful to the friends of the Hajar poems, those whom I know and those whom I do not know, who have engaged with the poems over the years, foremost among them Dr. Amina Wadud, Theodora Ranelli, and visual artist Hajjah Ann Saunders.

I am grateful to the following for first publication of some of the poems, or early versions of them:

"Hajar in America." *The Middle East Report and Information Project (MERIP)* 205 no. 27 (1997): 39.

"The Water of Hajar." *Ruah.* Berkeley, California: Dominican School of Philosophy & Theology 10 (2000): 10

"The First Thing." In *The Poetry of Arab Women, A Contemporary Anthology,* edited by Nathalie Handal, 140–44. Interlink, 2001.

"Hagar Writes a Letter to Sarah as a Cathartic Exercise Suggested by Her Therapist." *The Muslim World* 9 no. 1–2 (1999): 37–42.

"Isaac Wakes Up to Hajar and Ismaïl Terrorizing the House." *Publio* 3 (2008).

"Sarah's Laugh II," "Hajar's Ram," "Asiya Is Waiting for a Sign," and "Among the Midianites on U.S. 31." *Tiferet: A Journal of Spiritual Literature.*

"Little Mosque Poems" first appeared on the (since defunct) website, MuslimWakeUp!.com, 2004.

"Lifting the Hajar Heel." In *Language for a New Century: Contemporary Voices from the Middle East, Asia, and Beyond,* edited by Carolyn Forche, Ravi Shankar, Tina Chang, and Nathalie Handal, 84. New York: W.W. Norton, 2008. An earlier version of "Lifting the Hajar Heel" appeared in *Azizah.*

"Balqis Makes Solomon Sign a Pre-Nup." *Pakistani Journal of Women's Studies* (2004): 53–56.

"Most Wanted." In *Reclaiming Beauty for the Good of the World: Muslim & Christian Creativity*, edited by George Dardess and Peggy Rosenthal, 219. Louisville; KY: Fons Vitae, 2010. 219

"The Mihrab of the Mind." *The Atlanta Review* (2007): 37.

"Asiya's Aberrance." In *I Go to the Ruined Place: Contemporary Poems in Defense of Global Human Rights,* edited by Melissa Kwasny and M. L. Smoker, 55–57. Sandpoint, ID: Lost Horse Press, 2009.

"Not the Same." *Cyphers* 44 (1997): 14.

"Mary Calls Her Old High School Teacher from the University Library at 4 a.m." *Cyphers* 45 (1998): 42–43.

CONTENTS

ii.

iii.

i.

The Water of Hajar

After the searing light
After abandonment
After the blow
that brings the head to the ground
and breaks the teeth
After the unrelenting vision
After the god who requires blood and obedience,
how do you find water?

It has no content
It is the cupping of the face
It is the wiping of the forehead
It cools the lips
and moves without words
It is almost not visible
between thorn and rocks

Where on this earth
is the water of Hajar
the water that came
up from the ground,
from the ground of Hajar

given
freely, freely
by the God of Hajar

The First Thing

I am Hagar the immigrant

There came to me the revelation
of the water

I left the world of Abraham,
jugs sealed with cork,
cooking-grease jars,
Sarah's careful kitchen fires

I walked across a razor-sharp horizon,
slates of earth, sediment
of ancient seas

to stand alone at this frontier:
where the shape of the cup of morning is strange
and dome of sky, mat of earth have shifted,
where God does not have a house yet
and the times for prayer have not been appointed,

where the only water is buried deep
under hard ground and I must find it
or my child will die, my people
remain unborn
The first thing
the founder does
is look for water

I am Hajar, mother
of a people
I stand here
straddling the end and the beginning

Each rock cuts into the heel like God
Each step is blood, is risk:

is prayer

Hajar, First Woman on the Moon

Abraham is a just dot now,
distant planet
Sarah's laughter floats by in globules
I grab, swallow one, laugh
I am alone in a space
no one else has ever inhabited

I'm not what I was before:
Not Sarah's Hajar,
nor Abraham's, not
a girl of Egypt anymore
Can't go back now

& I don't know
what else to be
What will anchor me?
I somersault like hiccups
There is too much noise on earth
to hear God there
In a life spent listening
to commandments, I never
had the luxury
of this lunar silence

Things whiz by. Djinns swing
from galactic chandeliers,
eavesdropping

Was that a ram?
Was that a lote tree?
I hear the beating of many wings
& someone being taken on a tour of heaven
Will these weightless shapes
be hewn into a cube
solid enough to anchor earth?
Did I touch that rock before?
Seven times?

Hajar in America

We came over together
I spoke no English
He had a mission:
grad school, then it's back to save the masses

Here I am now with the baby on my hip,
alone in Newark,
on foot, looking for milk at the all-night Exxon
I hear he's marrying her,
the teaching assistant with the frosted hair

I have to learn how to drive

Professor and Mrs. Abraham

You were always typing up his papers,
Tending to his hunger and his thirst
You scheduled his appointments, edited
The memoirs of his spiritual search,

Of how he shook the stars and broke the moon,
Questioning the planets and the sun
For years, a rebel on the mountainside,
Iconoclast, until he found the one,

the God he was certain would not set
But Sarah, did you never have a thirst?
Did you ever take off on a quest?
Do you have a desert in you and despair,

To make you rail against the sun and stars?
Have you found a god who will not fail?
Or do you still bow to the customary god,
God of your fathers, tethered in your heart?

Hajar Writes a Letter to Sarah as a Cathartic Exercise Suggested by Her Therapist

Dear Sarah, life made us enemies
But it doesn't have to be that way.
What if we both ditched the old man?
He could have visitation rights with the boys
alternate weekends and holidays
(especially the Feast of the Sacrifice,
—he took that Day anyway,
forgetting it was about me in the desert
watching my baby dehydrate near to death).
Anyhow, you and I, we'd
set up house, raise the kids,
start a catering business maybe
You have brains. So do I.
We could travel. There are places to see
besides Ur and this nowheresville desert
with its tribes of hooligans

No. Your lips thin when you disapprove,
like the mother I almost remember
from before I wound up in your house.
I was barely more than a girl.
You used to laugh then. In those days,
you could stand to look at me. We
even hugged, sometimes.

Oh, Sarah, you need years of therapy.
Can't you admit that what he did was wrong?
Be angry at him—for just one second.

You don't have to be angry forever,
just long enough to know the world won't fall apart.
Long enough to pity him,
yourself, me
Laugh, Sarah, laugh
Imagine
God, the Possibility.
~~Sincerely~~ Love,
Hajar

Page Found Crumpled in the Wastebasket
by Hajar's Writing Desk

sarah you bitch,
you backstabbing woman
trotting after your husband
pinning the curtain up in the mosque
blindsiding other women
smacking the bad girls on the hands
saying *oh no sir we're not like them*
we don't want the vote
oh no sir we don't want the ERA
oh no brother we don't want to pray in the mosque
oh no sir we don't want equality
that would go 'gainst GAWD and nature
that would go 'gainst ALLAAH and the prophet
that would lead straight to permissive sex illicit drugs
immorality and the ruination of families
you mealy mouthed bitch
you House Negro of womankind
you gutless spineless toothless truthless
partial-birth abortion of a woman
you dried-up old—

Kin

Sarah, you massaged my sacrum
with a tennis ball when I was in labor.
Like a priestess of the body, you
wiped the newborn Ismail clean
of birthblood and whispered first
holy words into his ear. You are his mother
too. We are kin. No decrees
of man or God can make this truer
than it is, nor can it be cloven.

We did not begin with the husband we shared,
but in Egypt, with divine
intelligence arrowed from eye to eye
across a patio of pagan strangers,
when I was royalty and you were trembling
in the house. You knew exile and I
knew exile. You suffered and I suffered.

Like matter, kinship can be changed
but not destroyed. Cruelty tarnishes,
but cannot dissolve it. We are kin
from bread baked together,
salted, broken, eaten, sacred
as a challah braid at sunset on the Night of Power;
from the battering waters of the sea we crossed;
from the Tree of Life whose branches

we burned to stay alive. Kin
we are from knowledge of the Name;

you had the first letters, I had the last
and, putting them together, we
spelled out the Secret.

From Sarah's Egypt Diary

I see now. Either I play
the little woman shrunk to fit,
the sister when convenient—

for that price, I get a stunted sort of love
and safety, which is not the same
as heart-serenity—

Or, free in my body and my mind,
I leave Ibrahim open to attack
from tribes who'd pen us for the kill,

the tyrant king, even our own community,
where some will say my husband's not a man
for not controlling me.

Either way, I lose.
But I refuse.

You are cheats, your bargains frauds.
Your scales are weighted,
you who profit by this power—

I refuse to buy and sell
I refuse to trade with you.

Sarah's Laugh II

... and she laughed. But We gave her glad tidings of Isaac ...
She said, "Alas for me, shall I bear a child,
seeing I am an old woman ..."

Quran: Hud, 11:71–72

I think I get it now
Stories aren't over till they're over
The meaning changes as the narrative unfolds
Ishmael had to come before Isaac
Hagar had to pass through my life

She was my trial and my crucible
I failed miserably
I put her out like a cat
with her helpless young
I forsook Hagar when she most needed me

But Isaac came anyway,
to make me as ungainly as Hagar and as vulnerable
to make my body plump and firm like hers
to remind me of her body and her moves
and of the temporary sisterhood of pregnant women

Isaac came to play and replay
the Hagar videos for me
Isaac came to squawk like Ishmael
when Ishmael kept us up nights
and I wished to God they'd both go away

Then I became the patient one like Hajar
Understanding welled up in me like milk
when Isaac came, like grace unbidden
Grace has this trick of coming unbidden
This is cause for laughter

Hajar's Ram

Ibrahim's sacrifice of Ismaïl
was averted by a miracle, revealed
to be a temporary trial of his faith,
but Sarah sacrificed Hajar for real
Where was Hajar's ram?
No divine cavalry galloped over dale
at the eleventh hour to say,
don't throw her out—
This was a test. This was only
a test.

Maybe Hajar's ram was the miracle
of the rest of her life. First finding
the will to live, cut off and alone,
then foraging in the desert
for a new sort of family,
one not based on lineage or ownership
or an identity foisted on you like a mask,

but the kind of family that sticks with you
even when you become pariah
The patient threading of relationship,
the lifelong piecework of love—
The growth of friendship, slow
and thorny like a desert rhizome.
with its rare and wondrous blooms—
Maybe her ram was all of these
Maybe her miracle was human being

Isaac Wakes Up to Ismaïl and Hagar Terrorizing the House

It is not permissible that the authors of devastation
should also be innocent.

—JAMES BALDWIN, *The Fire Next Time*

This crazy black woman banging on our door,
and her glowering bearded brown son behind her, scare me.
They don't belong here. Can't they see
they are disturbing my homeland security?

The first time these strangers surfaced,
Mama fainted at the screen door
and my father sat me down:
"Son, there's a trifling thing we haven't told you.
There was no room for it in our curriculum.
. . . so you see, this woman was—just a blip in our story.
No pledges were made that needed keeping.
What they say's not true; do not believe it.
They are crafty, they are taught from birth to lie.
We are still the decent folk you know.
It's all them; they are incapable of modern life.
The other one, well, yes, he is your brother,
technically—but estranged. We deny
any living family tie."

"But—but why do they hate us?"
I almost cried, eyes big and shining.

A hole gaped beneath me, full of monsters.
Mama squeezed my hand. "Don't worry.
You don't ever have to know them.
We have made this lovely shell for you,
called 'our quality of life.'
This must go on unbroken.
Our barges full of garbage must stay free
to plow their stately courses on the sea.
Do not let doubts across the border.
Not a single trip to Burger Land
will we compromise."

Still. Sometimes I hear their keening
under the hum of our fridge or my tv.
"Lies, all lies," I tell myself,
but I don't know if the noises
getting louder are outside the house
or inside my head,
a terroristic truth destroying me.

Hagar No Roses

I only understood Hagar when my baby got a fever
It was late & we were just off Medicaid
& above the poverty line but not enough
for insurance plans or private doctors.
It was my first baby. I didn't know
when not to worry. I knew high fevers
could damage brains if left too long.
I knew the little body felt wrong,
shook slightly, eyes rolled back,
not responding to acetaminophen.
The on-call at the ER was busy,
didn't phone back for what seemed like hours
while I paced like Ethiopian Hagar in her desert
watching Ismaïl's small sunken chest
gasp up & down in throes of thirst.
Hagar did not slump over the body
waiting for what grace might come—
she shook her fist at the angel: *Help us.*
It was not a plea, but a demand.

I went through lists of people I knew
—who would know what to do for babies?
who willing to wake to worry with me?—
wringing the bouquets of useless roses
they'd laid at the foot of motherhood
I hated knowing I would humble myself

to phone them in the middle of the night,
to stand with arms down by my side
however long, whatever their conditions,
if they would tell me what the baby needed *now*.

Hagar, no roses here—
Motherhood is bitter fighting
against death-forces
in a desert of indifference.
Provide water! Provide balm
If there is any salve in the world,

it is for this, here, now: the infant, small flames
that rise in irises to flicker like tigers.

Hajar at the AIDS March

—O son of Adam! I fell ill but you visited Me not.
—How could I visit You, when You are the Lord of the worlds?
—Did you not know that My servant was sick but you visited
him not? Did you not know that if you had visited him,
you would have found Me by him?

—From a hadith qudsi of the Prophet Muhammad

The mosque board members
examine the dogma ID card
of every supplicant at the door,
run morality background checks
on the impoverished and the ill.

In the desert, with the boy dying,
Hajar ran to the heights.

Faith acts
in her hands and feet.

This matters: the firm flesh of now,
the head in the crook of the arm,
the downy notch of beauty,
this world of God.
Hajar is out
marching
in the AIDS rally today.

1996

Hajar's Sandals

"Behold, Safa and Marwa are among the symbols of God."

Quran: The Cow, 2:158

Hajar wedges her shoulder
between ledge of sky
and slate of earth
to save, from a crushing fate,
herself and her son.

We call the earth that mounds
around her sandals
Safa and Marwa.
Holy, these, God says:
Honor your mother's feet.

Over the lava-rock land,
people settle, hardening
into tribes and loyalties—
walking in the grooves of Hajar's sandals
and forgetting Hajar's ordeal.

The Caseworker Visits Abraham and Sarah

I am here to investigate reports of—
—No, sir, it is not okay.
—No, ma'am, it is not his right.
We call it abuse.
—I don't care what your ancient culture says
about the body of the woman in your bond.
—I don't care what your modern Zionism says
about your right to own the body of the land.
Neither of you will get by anymore
on tribe or tradition left unquestioned.
You will not be left in peace, if this is peace.
It is time for you to pause, if you have conscience.
It is time to face the awful truth.
No state of shelter, this, for any soul.

Hagar Dreamwork: The Therapist's Notes

You've got this Hagar thing all wrong
It's mythic. You're stuck
at left-wing literal levels
of rage-for-justice rhetoric
and knee-jerk feminist bludgeoning
Go get your Jung and Ibn al-Arabi;
What is the Hagar function in the psyche?
Here we have the angel and the baby;
here, two wives, two brothers,
a doppelganger story.
It's all interior, desert and city,
mountain and well.
Take it away from history;
wake up and jot down the latest jigsaw clue:
All the characters in the Hagar dream are you.

At the Snowcap

Behold, Abraham said, "My lord, show me how thou givest
life to the dead." He said "Dost thou not then believe?"
He said "Yea, but to satisfy my own heart." He said,
"Take four birds, tie them, then put a portion of them
on every mountain, then call to them:
They will come to thee with speed."

QURAN: The Cow, 2:260

Despair, tear me
like a quartered bird,
fling each carrion piece on a mountaintop

Wind, blow
in the four directions of pain:
grief, anger, harm, hate

Who is the one
who can restore?
Love, resurrect my small beating heart—

I fly to you from the four directions,
bird, bird
once more

The Fire of Hajar II

O Fire, be thou cool and safe . . .

QURAN: The Prophets, 21:69

Tears wet my beard. I looked back, but she was gone.
I have not been spared, this time, from the fire,

this pain that burns my heart in leaving Hajar
and the child. God once cooled a blazing fire

And made it safe for me when, in my youth,
I blazed for truth and burned a path afire

Now this lava desert is her path, her trial.
Be thou safe and cool for Hajar, fire!

Postcards from Hajar,
a Correspondence in Four Parts

*"O our Lord, I have made some of my family to dwell in a
valley without cultivation by your sacred House . . . so fill the
hearts of some people with love for them, and provide fruit for
them that they may give thanks"—the prayer of Abraham*

QURAN: Ibrahim, 14:37

i.

Ismaïl and I made it,
in case you're wondering.
Been learning the basics
of wilderness survival.
Weather very hot here,
but it's a dry heat,
bearable
once you find a water supply.
Angel Gabe dropped by,
fixed plumbing
so we have a well.
We're invited to the Jurhum's tonight
for dinner with the tribe.
Their girl is Ismaïl's age.
Tell Sarah I said—
oh, never mind.
Regards,
Hajar
P.S. I have decided to found a nation.

ii.

Sarah's pregnant, can you believe it!
Wish you were here
to talk her through the birth.
We often think of you
and how it used to be
when you and the baby were with us.
It wasn't so bad, was it? Helpmeet
you were, to a lonely aging couple,
and so bright you filled the house.
Glad to know you two survived
abandonme—er, being in the desert.
Nice to hear about the water and all.
A nation, huh? Well, you take care.
Hugs to Ismaïl. Write back soon!
Fondly, your ex,
Abraham

iii.

The baby is moving.
I'm too old for this! (laughing)
I will teach him to love his big brother.
Maybe one day they will
make up for their mothers.
Look, I'm sorry things went the way
they did between us, Hajar.
It just wasn't working.
In the end, it was my marriage and
I had to save it. I am relieved
things are all right for you

over there in that—that distant
—well, that place where you went.
You and your son will always
have a place in my regard.
Sincerely,
Sarah

iv.

Been busier and busier, hard
to find time to write, what with
our new city, my responsibilities
as founding mother.
Ismaïl sends love to baby
brother Isaac (congratulations!).
Sarah, yes, breastfeeding is tough
on nipples at first, but keep at it.
You will see in his brown eyes
dreams of warm milk
and still the hoarse hyena
of a deadly hunger.
Abraham, if you do
drop by sometime, we
may well have increased
like unto the starry sky
and multiplied.
Peace,
Hajar

The Threshold

"Change the threshold of your gate."
—A traveler, refused hospitality by Ismaïl's wife,
left this message. Recognizing it to be from his father,
Ismaïl divorced her and sought another spouse.

—From a hadith of the Prophet Muhammad in Sahih Bukhari

Because I came to her door
as an old man without a tribe,
a verb outside the sentence of her nation,
she stood on the polished stone
threshold and denied
a small water jug to me.

Parched, I did not say
"I am kin."
There are those you cannot teach.

Change your threshold
until you can embrace
the stranger, the despised, and say
your father Abraham
came to visit you today.

All Good

They see it as far-off,
but We see it as near.

QURAN: The Ways of Ascent, 70:6–7

i.

Out in the blue infinitude
that reaches and touches us
sometimes, Hajar and Sarah
and Abraham work together
to dismantle the house of fear, brick
by back-breaking brick.
With a broom of their own weaving,
they sweep away the last remains.
They sit down for a meal
under the naked stars.

Ismaïl and Isaac come around shyly,
new and unlikely companions.
Hajar introduces them
to her second and third husbands
and a man from her pottery class
who is just a friend.
Hajar's twelve grandchildren
pick up Sarah's twelve at the airport.
The great-grandchildren appear,
set down their backpacks,
and tussle to put up the sleeping tents,
knowing there will be no more rams,
no more blood sacrifice.

ii.

Sorrows furrow every face.
This, in the firelight, no one denies.
No one tries to brush it all away
or rushes into glib forgiveness.
First, out of the woods, shadows emerge:
the dead of Deir Yassin,
killed by Zionist terror squads,
the Kiryat Menachim bus riders
killed by Palestinian suicide bomber.
They face each other, tense up.
Some of them still need gravestones.
The ghosts of Mahmoud Darwish
and Yehuda Amichai begin to teach them
how to pronounce each other's names
in Hebrew and in Arabic. The poets
will have a long night of it. Meanwhile,
a Hamas sniper, a Mosad assassin fall
to their knees, rocking; each one cries,
"I was only defending my—my—"
Into the arms of each,
Hajar and Sarah place a wailing
orphaned infant. Slow moaning
fills the air: Atone, atone.

iii.

The grieving goes on for ages.
When the orange groves are given back
to their rightful owners, the old family drama
finally loses its power, withers, dies. A telling time
for new stories begins. Housekeys
digging bloody stigmata into the palms
of Palestinians cast from their homes
turn into hammers and nails for the rebuilding.

Hajar pours water that becomes
a subtle, sweet, and heretofore unheard of wine.
Sarah laughs again, more deeply.
Abraham is radiant. Everyone, this time
around, can recognize
in the eyes of every other,
the flickering light of the Divine.

Knowing at Arafat

Hajj is Arafat.

—Prophet Muhammad, peace and blessings be upon him

The story goes, Arafah got its name
because Abraham learned from the Angel
the ritual stations of the Hajj, ending
on that mountaintop, where Gabriel
says, "Do you know your stations now?"
and Abraham says "Yes." And so
the plateau was called Arafah—"He knew."

Story two—there's always a story two—begins with Eve
falling to earth. Where she touched down
is called "Grandmother"—"Jeddah," in Arabic.
Eve wandered, seeking a face she knew.
"Adam, is that you?" And the plateau of reunion
where she found her love anew
is Arafat, meaning "She knew."

Both stories can be true:
One, through patient study
with the honored teacher, learns,
I have found my path.
The other journeys out into the world
and reaches the same sweet elevation:
Baby, I've found You!

The Kaba's Lap

A low brick ledge extends
the Kaba's perimeter
in a half-circle called the Hijr,
the "Lap." The Kaba used to be that big.
Entering the Lap breaks the count

of seven circlings
because it is not the path around,
but the path inside.
It is part of no ritual.
It is Kaba, and it is not.
Lore says Hajar and her son

are buried in the Kaba's Lap,
and so is a basket of green gems.
No one knows if this is true.
It is, and it is not.
The Kaba's Lap is a ghost limb,

our forgotten grandmother's arm,
reaching around to make haven
for the heartbroken, the tired,
the ones unable to keep circling with the crowd,
the orphans of the orphan's faith.

Lifting the Hajar Heel

Dying for water,
Hajar went racing
back and forth in the valley,

when what she needed most
was under the heel of her foot.
All it took was an angel's nudge.

Little self, panting in the world,
take a hint, lift your heel.
Find your own long-buried Zamzam spring.

Hajar Triumphant

Islam began as a stranger and will return as a stranger.

—Prophet Muhammad

Hajar *hajarat* Hajirah *hujirat*
We don't even know your name
Our Prophet traces his line
to a Black woman
whom we know
only by her function:
to migrate, to be abandoned,

holding out after hope of help
and home wholly vanish,
ha huna, ha ana, Here I Am,
Eve out of Eden,
left with only the *wahy** of water
and the task of helping another
human being, Ismaïl:
He who, without Hajar, is history

Hence, "*islam,*" "to surrender,"
begins with *hijrah,* alienation,
homo sapiens at ground zero,
cast out in otherhood, motherhood,
I and Thou in the desert,
having no hard rod of law to lean on for holiness,
but only this flow between our fingers

---

*wahy: divine revelation.

Hajar Enters the Garden,
Well-Pleased and Well-Pleasing

O Self reassured,
return to your Lord
gratified and gratifying.
Come in among my worshipers
and in my garden, enter.

QURAN: Dawn, 89: 27–30

It happened in gymnastic splay,
my limbs double-helixed, spiraling
into climax after climax
I abandoned myself
I abandoned the stars, moon, and sun
I do not like the ones that set
My Hajar-heart sizzled to its coil
I took reality inside me,
carried the Soul of God in my womb
God couldn't have abandoned me if he tried

It is not about the tucked head of a handmaid
or the ferality of a mother
It is not the story of wifely submission—
not the way you like it
If you plod mule-like over my trail,
you will get only sore pilgrim feet
Bypass Hajar of the thirsty child
Go beyond Hajar the water seeker
Water and dust became the same to me
Angel and child became one fetal curl

My bellyskin became transparent
I saw worlds upon worlds in it
Onyx cities, obelisks towering
Fields of wheat, pond fish
Seven fat kine and seven lean tractors
Faces, male and female, sweating in labor
Famine, slave-trading, cattle cars
Giant mills grinding human bones
Small fierce hatreds swelling rivers with corpses

This too is allowed to slake its thirst
This too is allowed by God the Killer
God the Tsunami, the Leveler,
God the Loving, the Breastgiver
All of it, good and evil, from God

And this too is allowed:
Love growing like a soft maze in my pussy
Wriggling shining with blood brown babies born loved
Matted and licked like kittens,
the poor and the pampered alike, the girl and the boy alike,
born into new worlds destroyed by old
All of it exists, all of it now, all of it in this desert
that is not a desert if you see mitochondrially
Fronds turning tendrils, Eve's garden returning

I did not run between Safa and Marwa, I dove twisting in air
I saw Eve's first footprints, big as brontosaurus
I backstroked from mountain to mountain,

a sea-horse shaped fetus in belly fluid
Seven-time-seven times born and reborn
Faith and doubt and despair and faith again
And the state in which faith and doubt double back
and copulate and enter each other
unforgivably and rocking and pulling come together,

back into nucleotidal darkness
where a tongue of light, yellow stamen
in a dark purple iris unfurling   let there be
let there be   let there be
And I Am
I thin into amniotic gel
and coat the universe,
pure Being

This,
and I cried, "I am pleased with God"
God couldn't abandon Me if he tried.

Hagar Begone

Sometimes I wish Hagar would stop
dogging my steps
I wish I'd never heard
of the whole tribe—
the jealous, quarreling women,
the God-obsessed patriarch,
the vying sons,
and both their whiny progenies
The messy soap opera
of Middle Eastern religion
is not the center of the world

Maybe I'll make my next volume of poetry
about Norse mythology,
something completely icy and blond,
like an Ingmar Bergman film
There will be no hot desert ground in it
Passionate drama will be held in check
in favor of irony and form,
like in an MFA program

Or maybe I'll move the center of my consciousness
to some remote island
Ibn Battuta never visited
where the women and the men
go naked and love in the open
and have never even heard of underpants
much less the veil
You're finished here, Hajar!

Hajar Thorn

Hajar, I didn't mean begone
Visit me anytime, sit on my porch
I will make you strong dark tea
I will take you to Hot Springs, Arkansas
to see the mineral wells
so you can say, "Yes,
I have seen me some springs in my day"

Hajar, you will be betrayed over and over
It is your story
and I am complicit in it

Your brown hands will cup,
bringing water to Ismaïl
in his hoarse despair
curled, catatonic, naked,
covered with dust on the baked ground
sand driven even into the spaces
between one eyelash and the next

Hajar, even if I fail again and again,
you have been my guide
through a merciless, burning day
My sister, my teacher, my friend,
whether near to me or estranged,
inextractable thorn in my flesh

ii.

Asiya Is Waiting for a Sign

Then the family of Pharaoh picked him up (from the river).
The wife of Pharaoh said,
"A joy of the eye, for me
and for thee: Slay him not . . ."

<small>QURAN</small>: The Narration, 28:8–9

She paces Pharaoh's estate,
marble steps, the bristling tops of trees.
She is restless in her routine.
Couples arrive. She scans their faces,
and the oil stains under the Pharaoh's SUV.

Every day the headlines scream
plagues, locusts. Another naked child explodes
himself in the market, a frog croaks,
startles soldiers armed to the teeth.
Asiya sits at Pharaoh's dinner table

with the neo-conservatives nightly.
Why do they hate us? A mystery.
Asiya twitches, passes the paté.
That they slave to build us pyramids
is only free market forces at play.

The salmon is delicious. We
are entitled to the treasures
of the desert, and to dine in peace.
Asiya fidgets with her blue earring,
lapis lazuli. What is wrong with me,

she thinks. She slips away from husband,
guests, to the back porch by herself,
and scans the blue shining serpentine
river for a twitch, a movement,
for a basket in the reeds.

Asiya's Aberrance (*Nushuz Asiya*)

"O my Lord, build for me a house near You in the Garden,
and save me from Pharaoh and his doings,
and save me from the people who oppress."

—The prayer of Asiya, surrogate mother of Moses.
QURAN: Prohibition, 66:11

These chariot horses are flying
away from me
The world hurtles by
at frightening speed
Bodies explode in mid-air
Pyramids come crashing down into dust
Children are deliberately slaughtered
Homes with people living in them
are purposely demolished
Men are blindfolded leashed
in the name of freedom
People use the altars of the gods
to pray for killing

I don't understand this world
I want to build myself a house
in another sort of world
I wake from one of my nightmares
Pharaoh says, why are you screaming?
You have everything you ever wanted
Then he laughs and turns into a river of blood,
a snake crawling up my thigh
The nightmare isn't over, isn't over

The priests pray loudly for victory
They turn into frogs
They make disgusting noises
They look at me warily
The scholars and the teachers
explain why I am wrong
according to the laws
everybody knows
The newspapers call me a crazy woman,
a traitor, an apologist for terrorists,
a lesbian, a feminist, an anarchist,
an advocate for every brand of depravity

But it's Pharaoh who's crazy
It's the gods that accept
libations for murder
who are crazy
It's this upside-down order
of yours that's a danger to human life
I can't live in it anymore
Got to hold on
to these snorting horses
Got to get the reins back
Or they will break my neck
I'm going over
I'm going over
But not because I'm crazy

Daughter of the Pharisees

I am a daughter of the Pharisees
They have invented a religion unto themselves.
It has a logic like iron bars.
It has a law like a labyrinth,
inescapable, vast, every time I think
I have escaped it, I make a turn and
there it is, scything my steps.

I am the daughter of the Pharaoh
The shock of discovery is still fresh:
That there is a child in the river,
that it is not a sign of joy in Pharaoh's kingdom,
but one slender escape from a cruel order
imposed by ruthless men who are frightened inside.
What can I do but take the child, kiss and feed it,
and hope that one day it will bring down the walls around us.

The god I have worshiped is a false god,
but there is a god who flows
like blood through my veins,
like milk through my breasts,
slips through iron bars like secret nourishment
to Mary. So small, so ordinary, it passes
unnoticed by the Pharisees,
leaves the Pharaoh unimpressed
So divine, so potent, it creates within my ribcage
gardens upon gardens of the blessed.

The Last Day before Asiya's
Nervous Breakdown

The branch silhouetted against the sky frightens me
The books I used to read lie about me
The skeleton of a wet leaf
pressed against the pavement
makes me shudder. The lying books
are believed, and I am not believed

My self stumbles against sharp protrusions and curses me
This happens, then I make breakfast for the children
Then I drive to work in Pharaoh's order
Then I come home frightened
I am tired of being who I am in Pharaoh's order
May I stop now? May I be something else?
Would that offend my father the Pharaoh, or the ladies of the city?

The procedure of getting clean clothes
puzzles me for days
I don't know the first thing about living
All I have learned is wrong
I have to start again from the first step
This is a marvelous revelation
I hold it close like a newborn babe
Its cries frighten me
The high branch rasps like a threat

My balance in the bank is not correct
The people at the bank will not correct it for me.
It is Pharaoh's bank.
My page is torn in two like a parted sea
I somersault into the blank ripped space
between the things I used to believe,
and wake up not where I thought I was

The shape of the leaf is wrong
I miss the appointed times for prayer
I am always in the wrong place
This place is a river of blood. I scream
This terror targets everyone, like a sniper

I must at least make sure the children are safe
before I succumb
Where is a place of safety to put the children?
The branch against the sky heaves
like a heavy arm about to strike
I will try to pray now,
knees pressed tightly to my chest
There is too much hurt in the world to bear
What if there is no place?

Asiya Meets Miriam at the Riverbank

Miriam knows how much
depends on her
She steadies the basket
She braces herself to the task

Asiya meets her eye
across the riverbank
People of the palace wade
between them,

each with an opinion
Don't trust her
She's one of them
Call your guards

But Asiya has been waiting
for Miriam without knowing
who Miriam will be
Asiya lifts her arm

using what authority
she has left in Pharaoh's order
to clear the way
for Miriam's advance

Asiya knows Miriam
is a messenger
from the other side
of the riverbank

Their hands stretch
across the waters, each
grasping the fragility
of what will save them

The Red Fish

Behold, Moses said to his attendant,
I will not give up until I find
the junction of the two seas, or spend ages in travel.
But when they reached the junction, they forgot their fish,
which took its course through the sea as through a tunnel.

QURAN: The Cave, 19:60–61

I am ready to stop hovering
at the meeting of the two seas
I am ready to cut through the waters
with my clean body
and swim after the red fish

I followed the directions they gave me in the city
but I have not found the way,
nor have I met the wise one
supposed to guide me in the wild

When will the great fish surface?
Tell her I am here at the fork in the waters,
ready to grasp the fin
and swim into the turquoise life

I have been living under a sky
lower than the real sky
No wonder I am stooped
No wonder it hurts to stretch straight and dive

This is the land I know:
Mean huts, harsh but sheltering
Outside them are fears thick as trees and doubts
that litter the ground to trip my feet
What if this unripe persimmon
is the only fruit we're meant to eat?

The world is tender under today's sky, bruised;
I want to learn how to brush my skin against its skin
I am laying my clothes on the rock now
Am I naked enough yet?

The first breath in water hurts the lungs
Where are you, teacher? Are you almost here?
And what if I am wrong again?
What if there are no rubied caverns undersea?
—where is that no-show guide?
I shiver, doubt, pull my clothes back on
half-fastened, awry

Here I am, at the estuary of the two waters
pacing from tree to stunted tree
looking for the sign of a great fish,
and not seeing what I see

Arab and Hebrew Flow and Cross Over

Arab and Hebrew
come from the same root,
the letter *'ayn*,
which means the "eye."

"Arab" means "the flow"
and "Ebri" means "the crossing over."
Think of a river:
both meanings apply.

If you know one
but not the other,
you might at least
see your way over; try.

Among the Midianites on U.S. 31

"O my dear father, hire him—truly the best of men
for thee to hire is the man who strong and trusty"
—the Midianite maiden

QURAN: The Narration, 28:26

He parts the uncouth crowd like butter
and says in his sexy growl,
"Let the ladies through,"
gesturing with his sunglasses up the street
to where the two sisters' little Geo is parked—
so much for Moses keeping a low profile
among the Midianites.
"Would you like an escort home?" he asks.
"Thanks, we're fine," the older sister says.
"Yes, so many nutjobs out at this hour,"
the younger one says at the same time,
pinching her elder on the arm hard,
and watching him in his black leather jacket
(butter again) swing a leg over his motorcycle.
"He is so buff, I could die
and go to heaven right now,"
younger whispers. She's caught
the scent of metropolitan sophistication,
mystery, and maverick in his aftershave.
Throw in his brooding look, like a man
with a thorn in his paw and danger on his tail,
and those small-town boys at the pool hall

working part-time at the Kmart
don't stand a chance. That evening
she leans toward her father in his armchair.
"Daddy," she says winsomely,
"didn't you say you need a man
to help you at the gas station?"

Balqis Makes Solomon Sign a Pre-Nup

"We have been taught the speech of birds
and have been given of every
thing. This is indeed Grace manifest."
—Solomon

QURAN: The Ants, 27:18

I love you,
but I won't be
signing off
my sovereignty.

I come to you
but keep my throne
for my Self's
ascent alone.

Don't pull that mystic
oneness stuff—
that I love you
is enough.

I shower you
with peacock gifts,
my silken body—
mine to give.

Don't ask the hoopoe
how late I'll be—

I cherish
living free.

Other wives
surrendered more?
You've not loved
a queen before.

All yields to you,
golden prince,
bird speech, ant worlds—
all but this.

Zuleikha Ionic

"Nor do I absolve my own self; the self commands to evil,
unless my Lord bestow his Mercy—
truly my Lord is Forgiving, Full of Mercy."
—Zuleikha

Quran: Joseph, 12:53

This is Zuleikha:
Love surges beautiful
high voltages in her
She is loose, frightened,
charring everything
she touches and
hurting, hurting, hurting
herself

Zuleikha, ionic,
charged electrically
from an excess
of passion, or a deficiency

She is a lover
She is a lover
She doesn't know how to stop it

This is Yusuf:
He is a conductor
Zuleikha doesn't know from conductor
She wants to surge
She wants him to surge with her
She doesn't have patience for science
She breaks the beakers and sweeps the table clean

She knocks over the gallon and lights the gasoline
Zuleikha: Love is pyromania

She wants to galvanize
every particle known
to man, woman, God

Tonight she is cobalt flame
leaping bluegold glorious to sky
Tomorrow she will be lying
in a heap, sobbing
in the grime of spent fire

Yusuf, scorched,
will have left
sometime in the night

He will not curse her
She is a lover
One day she will learn
the science of conduction,
how to love and not be consumed

Then she will become
the spark itself and bond
to every blue and particle of gold,
to all that is Yusuf in the world,
spinning, sub-atomic,

alight in beauty
alight in beauty

Zuleikha Tantra

"Zuleikha's a slut," the tabloids say.
The ladies of the city gloat
over her fall for handsome Yusuf.
Imams use her as a cautionary tale
in their Friday sermons.
No one wants their daughter
to turn out like Zuleikha,
prowling the bars for Yusuf's face,
craving a fix, a lay, a razor,
anything that will take her
away from her Yusuf-less world
toward the Lote Tree, comfort,
closeness, the shining steed, the night journey
to the heavenly city,
bathing in the River Kothar,
ranks upon ranks of angels, choral music,
and a man's full-bodied baritone
calling out in the dark night that hovers
just above the street lamps,
Come to beauty, Come to love,
where heart hearkens to heart,
the palm cupping the chin like a holy chalice, the lips
kissing her clavicle with its vulnerable skin,
down between her breasts rising like gibbous moons,
the hands sliding down around her waist and hips
and lower and lower and higher and higher
Oh God and Revelation and stars and angels spinning
All is divine and one and whole and pure
and full of grace like Yusuf, and Zuleikha

is gasping "oh God oh no don't bring me down again
take me back—"
but there's only a naked bulb swinging from the ceiling
the plaster peeling,
and another man who is not Yusuf
pulling on his clothes, not looking at her
Sex is the only way
Zuleikha
knows how to pray

The Ladies of the City

When she heard of their malicious talk,
she sent for them and prepared a banquet for them.

QURAN: Joseph, 12:31

The Ladies of the City
cut the fallen woman,
pecking fleshbites
from their fresh kill.

They prowl in packs.
But there's a banquet waiting—
kumquats and small knives,
sharp as the soul's disquiet,

for the Ladies of the City.
Love enters by surprise; hands jerk—
thumbtips sliced to bone.

They too will bleed for Beauty
—if they're lucky,
the Ladies of the City.

The Zuleikha Hotline

Zuleikha, my Joseph's gone. I'm fumbling,
knocking over the candles you left
on the windowsill from the days
of your crazy love vigils.
Phone me, please, from ancient Egypt
or the poets' Persia, or whatever time zone
of divine and earthly love you're in.
Tell me I can find the key to seven locks,
tell me any esoteric mumbo jumbo.
After the cityfolk jeered
and turned against you in your dark night,
did you see the angel of beauty
and cut your breast like an orange?
Is that a fruit knife sliding
across my wrist or butterflies alighting?
With these glass-sliver tears that cut my eyes
in a thousand places, I can't see
beyond the hand in front of me,
I'm bumping into walls like a moth
into the glass encasing the flame,
hurt by my longing.
I see the girl I was,
petty and vile,
smashing the chalice
because she could not have it,
how I hate her. Zuleikha,
how many of my fingers must I char
to learn the alchemy
of my Self?

Mary Phones Her Old High School Teacher from the University Library at 4 a.m.

"To the care of Zekariah was she assigned . . ."

Quran: The Family of Imran, 3:37

—No I am awake, Mary,
have been listening
for this call

—Yes, you
will bring forth
beauty

I, Zekariah,
always knew

—By the stir
of your head above
the flame. Bowed
over bunsen burner,
even then your lamp-
light was blue

Yes, you—
Mary, don't cry
—I know
what they are saying
—You are not to let
the hatemongers
disturb you

Did God not
send forth a river
to wash your feet
and let the trees
bend low to shade
and comfort you?

—You are standing
in what deep
rift?
You have drunk the milk of sky
and feel a sweet grace
unfurling in your belly
and it hurts?

Look up, Mary!
It was for this
I prepared you.
It will not hurt. Don't
glance back at me: Go
where angels beckon

Go into that blue-
gold flame

1991

Mary's Glade

And the pains of childbirth drove her to the trunk
of a palm tree. She cried, "Would that I had died before
this and been a thing forgotten and out of sight!" But a voice
from beneath called to her, "Grieve not! For your Lord
has provided a rivulet beneath you. And shake towards
yourself the trunk of the palm tree: It will let fall fresh ripe
dates upon you. So eat and drink and cool your eye."

QURAN: Mary, 19:23–26

If I could find a glade for my despair
And hide myself like some forgotten thing
By some dead tree trunk equally despised
And hear no more, and none to hear from me,
Maryam, would water rush out from the spring?

What fruits would drop for me and what voice bid
Me drink, and eat, and live, Mary? From where
Would comfort come when I have none to give?
                              If I could find a glade

Like yours, Maryam, where palm fronds are made
To shield young friendless women from cruel eyes
And tenderly to give them holy shade
Tell me where to search for such a place
And would the palm leaves bend? Tell me, Mary,
                              If I could find a glade

1986

Not the Same

"O my Lord, I have delivered her a girl,
and God knows best what I have delivered,
and a girl is not the same as a boy. And I have named her Mary,
and I commend her and her posterity to Thy protection . . ."
—Mary's mother

QURAN: The Family of Imran, 3:36

Mary's mother was disappointed: A girl
is not the same as a boy
God, on the other hand, threw a party,
went all out: Got the angels
carrying trays of light into her chamber,
clusters of nebulae like cold grapes,
sweetmeats to flutter in her mouth like butterflies,
tall milkshakes from heaven
Boys, give them lightning and thunder
on the mountain, shake them up a little
Start them off scrabbling among the sheep
and carpenter's nails
But a girl! Enfold her in linens luminous,
set the legions of heaven, with their enormous
muscled wings, to embroidering,
for her reception, something of comfort and joy
Keep the angels up late lovingly
preparing midnight snacks of holy sustenance
for the apple-of-the-eye girlchild:
    Right graciously God did welcome Mary*

---

*Quran: 3:37

Riverbank

And so, when she carried him to her people,
they said "O, Mary! Truly a surprising thing hast thou done.
O sister of Aaron! Thy father was not a man of sin,
nor was thy mother a woman unchaste."

QURAN: Mary, 19:27–28

Maryam is pregnant and unwed.
The townspeople turn on her.
"Shame," is their rallying word. She wants to say,
"You don't know the end of this story,"
but the townspeople mock and turn away.

Maryam vows silence,
begins to speak only in signs,
like Zekariah her teacher before her.
Scribbles across her belly mark
pathways to other modes of being,
from the inside out.

Maryam takes a path to a tree beside a stream,
blessed, neither of this world nor of the other.
The tree lets fall its fresh ripe fruit for her.
The stream froths to cool her swollen feet.
A voice speaks to her from beneath.

Maryam begins to see
that worlds upon worlds exist,

that she is one of the canals between worlds.
Between the riverbank of hatred
and the riverbank of love,
Maryam gives birth.

She returns. She faces the townspeople,
a sign, carrying a sign, speaking in signs:
Peace, bearing peace in her arms, proclaiming peace.

The Food of Mary

Each time Zekariah entered her prayer chamber,
he found her supplied with sustenance. He said,
"O Mary, whence cometh this?" She said, "From God."

QURAN: The Family of Imran, 3:37

After hours in my seventh-floor municipal office,
I am working on revisions to the drainage code
alone like Mary high in her temple
staring at the blank blue screen that is my life

Mary tapping at the holy keyboard,
God sent her fully microwaveable meals
with Alfredo sauce manifest
I bang on the candy machine down the hall: Nothing.
It has eaten my paltry pieces of silver

Mary had a mentor in Zekariah,
who dropped in and taught her divine wisdom
whenever he wasn't on a vow of silence
but only burned-out Bill from computer services,
styrofoam cup loosely in hand with a little cold coffee left in it,
comes by my door, to mutter about the weather

Mary got a visitation from Gabriel
which helped clarify things like her task in the world
I get the cross-town courier in bicycle shorts, panting,

not so much to announce a virgin birth unto me,
as carrying a roll of blueprints under his arm

which I study religiously while eating
naught but stale chips
and a linty Lifesaver
The hour is late; my hunger groweth
O Mary, Mary, whence cometh my divine crumb?

Khadija Gets Her Groove Back

Dark are his eyes, thick are his lashes, husky is his voice,
bushy is his beard, long is his neck, well-built is he.
When silent, a gravity dignifies him, and when he talks,
he soars, his logic like pearls in a pattern. A branch
between two branches, he is the most blooming
of the three in appearance . . .

—From a verbal portrait of the Prophet Muhammad
by Um Ma'bad, a Meccan woman, 622 C.E.

So Khadija comes in to get her cornrows done—
she's all DKNY with padded shoulders,
the Madame C. J. Walker of her day,
founder and CEO of Khadija Enterprises,
seventh-century Arab businesswoman.
I do her hair all the time, mmm-hmm, and lately
she has this shine. Girlfriend, Khadija,
how is that new man working out,
the one you hired from the temp agency?

Like a blossoming bough between two branches
Like a virgin beauty with lowered lashes
Like a man who, when he talks with low
measured voice, pearls scatter from his lips
Like a brocade cloak that envelopes its wearer
Like a caravan heavy with the treasures of Byzantium
when it is first spotted wending its way across the town
and you have been expecting it for a long, long time,

she says to me,
oh honey,
he is working out
just fine.

Our Lady of the Sorrows

It is hard to find Fatima. Fatima's face
is always averted from the crowd.
Fatima's form, wrapped in its cloak,
is always receding to another place
Did she carry in her pelvic floor
the knowledge that her son Hussain
would die at Karbala, his body gored,
my Lady of the Sorrows, of the shroud?
Girl of ten, anxious for her hounded father,
her pinched face peering right and left,
picking through Mecca's crooked streets
among the sweaty backs of men the day
had made unmindful, forlorn, bereft
little mother even as a little daughter,
she appears at Trayvon's killer's trial,
shadows the crowd at Ferguson,
Fatima, shuddering, shouldering the pain
of every mother's son who will be slaughtered.

Aisha of the Pearls

One day, the clasp to everything breaks
A woman loses her necklace in the sand
She leaves the caravan and goes alone
to sift the sand for pearls

People content with outer forms
abandon her, never knowing
the curtained howdah is empty
She draws her black cloak around her

like a cave of meditation
The desert threatens to bury her
She begins to thread together
what is important

She finds and is found, like a bead
of sand. She rises and rides
back to the city, accompanied
by someone who knows the path

The people suspect her, the search,
the guide, the whole story of the pearls
The people say to her: Who are you?
She answers: I am she who is alive.

Aisha Fails the Good Housekeeping Seal

—Based on an incident in the life of Aisha

I fell asleep while kneading dough
and the goat ate it
It was the last flour in the bin
Muhammad shrugged and we fasted

I was not meant for baking bread
Give me the ingredients of wisdom
Now that is a dough I would knead

Aisha: The *Islamic Inquirer* exclusive

I was a child star
My parents signed a contract
It's hard to be the poster girl
for a new endeavor—
you, the public, the press,
you gossips like to turn on a girl, don't you
you want your girls perfect
like little porcelain gods

I made one mistake—
No, not the night I was stranded on Sunset Strip
with no ride, no money, no credit cards
and took a ride from the only guy who stopped
That was not my fault

I made one mistake:
My stance on the war
I did the round of talk shows,
rousing up leading men for war
I was ripped for war
I rode right into it
And it tore this nation apart

Decades later, when
the dogs of Burbank barked at me,
I had an epiphany:
I was wrong. Peace was the way.
It's been sixty years
and you're still after me
for all the things that don't matter
Peace and justice matter.

Breaking: Aisha Claims to Be Post-Feminism

—an Islamic Inquirer *exclusive*

I did whatever I did
because I believed it was right
I narrated hadith
because I shared a life
with the Prophet of God
and had a good memory.
I fought Ali because, at the time,
I thought it was right.
I corrected men of religion
when I heard them running out half-cocked
reporting hadiths they hadn't heard but halfway.

Truth doesn't care
if you're a woman or a man or something else.
You want feminist,
talk to Asma bint Yazid
She was always getting in everyone's face
about women's rights this, women's role that.
She went to that UN conference,
came back wanting all us Medina chicas
to form an NGO.
Me, I just believe
everyone is a human being
and deserves to be treated like one.
If you want to call that feminist,
knock yourself out.

You just want a label
You want a brand name like "Aisha"
to slap on your cause. Anyway,
why are you people always interviewing me?
You know what [takes mike clip off]
I've had it with this scene
[walks out]

Nusaiba at Uhud

I did not turn right nor left but I saw Nusaiba there
fighting on my behalf.

—Prophet Muhammad

Arrows at Uhud
Blood on the ground
Men leave the Prophet
Exposed in the rout

Enter Nusaiba, defending,
Now left, now right,
The whirl of this woman
filling his sight.

Shield-wielder, she used
No manly disguise
Not lacking in reason
Not lacking in rites

Blood on her breast
Blood on her thigh
Body of a woman
Blood like mine

1988

Bilal's Mother

No one recorded what she gasped
when the whip split her flesh.

No one left in this world
knows what boulders
were heaved upon her.

We have two versions of her name:
Umaimah or Hamamah, bint Subh.
Slave names? Who was she?

Many distinguished Meccan ladies
come later to the fold than she,
enter our classic texts with greater fame.

Not her lineage,
but her split skin
screams nobility.

1988

What Is Recorded of the Response of Ghazali's Wife on Being Informed by Her Husband the Great Theologian That He Was Quitting His Job, Leaving Her and Their Children, and Skipping Town to Find God and the Proper Worship Thereof

[Reading instructions:
Read title of poem;
maintain silence for at least 45 seconds;
thank your listeners.]

What al-Ghazali's Mother Commented on the View of Her Son the Eminent Theologian that Women's Natures Tend Not Toward Spiritual Heights but the Baser Elements of Worldly Life Such as Bearing and Nursing Children and the Muck of Cooking, Cleaning, and Sex for Their Husbands and/or Masters

[Reading instructions:
Read title of poem;
maintain silence for at least 45 seconds;
thank your listeners.]

iii.

The Black Stone of My Heart

"Remember that We made the House a foundation
for people, and a place of serenity."

QURAN: The Cow, 2:125

My inner Kaba crumbled. Who will come
to lift the Black Stone of my heart
      on a white sheet by its four corners?
My inner Kaba crumbled. Do you know
how I used to leap at the call to prayer
      as if a lover was walking past,
      all my white scarves fluttering,
before my inner Kaba crumbled? Now I go
through the motions, hoping someone will come
      to lift the Black Stone of my heart

From a Former Grad Student
of Imam Ibn al-Qayyim

I've kicked aside my prayer rug
and decided to pray on the rushing river
I've smashed those pinchy little spectacles
I used to need to read exegesis,
and decided to read the lightning
crackling in the horizon and the psyche
I've kissed the red lipstick of poetry
and lit the cigarette of my soul
I've traded in my *zikr* beads
for the strappy high heels of ecstasy
Baby, I'm going out to get high on Love
and drunk at the Bar of Crazy Beauty,
so if any of those bearded *qazi* friends of yours
come around with their law books, tell them
I'll be dancing till white threads the black dawn

The Near Eastern Goddess Alumnae Office...

... hired me
to find out where have all the goddesses gone
whose hair ran down like wine.
I tracked down Isis
incognito on Cyprus.
She told me Ishtar
lived under the radar
in southern Iraq for years,
one step ahead of Saddam
She got sick under sanctions
and was killed
in the U.S. invasion by bomb.

Inanna ran a
dissident paper for years
in Syria, underground,
before the Baath ran her down.

Shekeena's been a
recluse, since she was disfigured
in an Israeli prison
during the first intifadah.

Hathor has her
Green Card, and the anti-depressant
dosage needed to maintain
a McReality consumer in the U.S. suburbs.

Ninsun, on the run,
took me aside and said,

We've been on the lam
for thousands of years,
rabbis, churchmen, and ulema
nipping our heels.
Caliph-kings and presidents
now tear off, now nail on, our veils.
Soldiers rape our daughters
and cut our sacred trees.
It's been a long time, girl,
since men knelt at the altar
of the feminine divine.
We gird our Selves for our comeback.
Meanwhile, the odd worshiper remains:
wherever the sex is good
and guys give head
(It's the least they can do,
considering, the goddess said),
where water and air are pollutant-free,
and human rights upheld.

The Mihrab* of the Mind

I'm told that we belong to different faiths
and pray at differing appointed times
to Gods of different names
We find comfort in familiar forms,
and each soul melts its candle
alone in its dark night

But I know this: our bodies' shapes divine,
these columns of flesh, this warm breath
of heart-talk between us,
these contain the covenant
God put at the base of Eve and Adam's spine

This is what religion is.
Its Kaba is the heart
Its prophet, savior, and messiah
is the nobler self
Its scriptures are always being written
in the here and now.

We are all its chosen tribe
Its miracle is joy; its fruit is gratitude.
Its holiest of holies has been placed
in the living church inside my chest,
in the mihrab of your mind.

---

*mihrab: the niche in the front wall of a mosque's prayer hall
indicating the direction faced in prayer.

Most Wanted

Warning: God has slipped the noose.
We must confirm the worst
of our righteous fears—
God has escaped the mosque,
the synagogue, the church
where we've locked up God for years.
We repeat unto you:

God is on the loose.

Henceforth beware:
You may find God in heathen beauty.
You may stumble upon God unaware.
Take appropriate measures:
You may have to behave
as if each human being
could reflect God's Face.

Tortoise Prayer

You think I'm lost to God because
you do not see me with the congregation
at the appointed prayer times
Where am I? I am learning

to give my life over, bit by bit,
to what is sacred. It is hard
My ego snaps like a piranha
Sometimes I feed it too well,

chomping the toes
of whoever irks me. Those
are mistakes. So you assume
I'm not a runner in the chase

for the Divine Face
But I may be a tortoise
to your hare. Don't be too sure
your fleetfoot pieties

are taking you there
faster than my plodding
and unlikely
kind of prayer

Little Mosque Poems

In my little mosque
there is no room for me
to pray. I am
turned away faithfully
five
times a day

My little mosque:
so meager
in resources, yet
so eager
to turn away
a woman
or a stranger

My little mosque
is penniless, behind on rent
Yet it is rich in anger—
every Friday, coins of hate
are generously spent

My little mosque is poor yet
every week we are asked to give
to buy another curtain
to partition off the women,
or to pave another parking space

I go to the Mosque of the Righteous
I have been going there all my life

I have been the Cheerleader of the Righteous Team
I have mocked the visiting teams cruelly
I am the worst of those I complain about:
I am a former Miss Mosque Banality

I would like to build
a little mosque
without a dome
or minaret
I'd hang a sign
over the door:
Bad Muslims
welcome here
Come in, listen
to some music,
sharpen
the soul's longing,
have a cigarette

I went to the mosque
when no one was there
and startled two angels
coming out of a broom closet
"Are they gone now?" one said.
They looked relieved

My great big mosque
has a chandelier
big as a Christmas tree

and a jealously guarded
lock and key.
I wonder why
everyone in it
looks just like me

My little mosque
has a bouncer at the door
You have to look pious
to get in

My little mosque
has a big sense of humor
Not

I went to the mosque
when no one was there
The prayer space was soft and serene
I heard a sound like lonely singing
or quiet sobbing
I looked around
A little Quran
on a low shelf
was reciting itself

My little mosque has a Persian carpet
depicting trees of paradise
in the men's section, which you enter
through a lovely classical arch
The women's section features—
well, nothing.

Piety dictates that men enter
my little mosque through magnificent columns.
Piety dictates
that women enter
my little mosque
through the back alley,
just past the crack junkie here
and over these fallen garbage cans

My little mosque used to be democratic
with a rotating imam
we chose from among us every month
Now my little mosque has an appointed imam
trained abroad
No one can deny his superior knowledge

We used to use our minds
to understand Quran
My little mosque discourages
that sort of hodge-podge these days
We have official salaried translators
for God

I used to carry around a little mosque
in the chambers of my heart
but it is closed indefinitely pending
extensive structural repairs

I miss having a mosque,
driving by and seeing cars lining the streets,
people double-parking, desperate

to catch the prayer in time
I miss noticing, as they dodge across traffic
toward the mosque entrance between
buses and trucks,
their long chemises fluttering,
that trail of gorgeous fabrics Muslims leave,
gossamer, the colors of hot lava, fantastic shades
from the glorious baked places of the earth
I miss the stiff, uncomfortable men
looking anywhere but at me when they meet me,
and the double-faced women
full of judgment, and their beautiful
children shining
with my children. I do.

I don't dream of a perfect mosque
I just want roomfuls of people to kiss every week
with the kisses of Prayer and Serenity,
and a fat, multi-trunked tree
collecting us loosely for a minute under
its alive and quivering canopy

Once, God applied
for a janitor position at our mosque,
but the board turned him down
because he wasn't a practicing
Muslim

Once a woman entered
my little mosque
with a broken arm,

a broken heart,
and a very short skirt
Everyone rushed over to her
to make sure
she was going to cover her legs

Marshmallows are banned
from my little mosque
because they might
contain gelatin derived from pork enzymes
but banality is not banned,
and yet verily,
banality is worse than marshmallows

Music is banned
at my little mosque
because it is played on
the devil's stringed instruments,
although a little music
softens the soul
and lo, a hardened soul
is the devil's taut drumskin

Once an ignorant Bedouin
got up and started to pee against a wall
in the Prophet's Mosque in Medina
The pious protective Companions leapt
to beat him
The Prophet bade them stop
A man is entitled to finish a piss
even if he is an uncouth idiot,

and there are things
more important in a mosque than ritual purity

My little mosque thinks
the story I just narrated
cannot possibly be true
and a poet like me cannot possibly
have studied Sahih al-Bukhari

My little mosque
thinks a poem like this must be
written by the Devil
in cahoots with the Zionists,
NATO, and the current U.S. administration,
as part of the Worldwide Orientalist Plot
to Discredit Islam
Don't they know
at my little mosque
that this is a poem
written in the mirror
by a lover?

My little mosque
is fearful to protect itself
from the bricks of bigots
through its window
Doesn't my little mosque know
the way to protect its windows
is to open its doors?

I know the bricks of bigots
are real
I wish I could protect my little mosque
with my body as a shield

I love my dysfunctional little mosque
even though I can't stand it

My little mosque loves Arab men
with pure accents and beards
Everyone else is welcome
as long as
they understand that Real Islam
has to come from an Arab man

My little mosque loves Indian
and Pakistani men with Maududi in their pockets
Everyone else is welcome because as we all know
there is no discrimination in Islam

My little mosque loves women
who know that Islam liberated them
fourteen hundred years ago and so
they should live like seventh-century Arabian women
or at least dress
like pre-industrial pre-colonial women
although
men can adjust with the times

My little mosque loves converts
especially white men and women

who give "Why I embraced Islam" lectures
to be trotted out as trophies
by the Muslim pom-pom squad
of Religious One-upmanship

My little mosque faints at the sight
of pale Bosnian women suffering
across the sea
Black women suffering
across the street
do not move
my little mosque much

I would like to find a little mosque
where my Christian grandmother
and my Jewish great-uncle the rebbe
and my Buddhist cousin
and my Hindu neighbor
would be as welcome
as my staunchly Muslim mom and dad

My little mosque has young men and women
who have nice cars, nice homes, expensive educations,
and think they are the righteous rageful
Victims of the World Persecution

My little mosque offers courses on
the Basics of Islamic Cognitive Dissonance.
"There is no racism in Islam" means
we won't talk about it

"Islam is unity" means
shuttup.
There's so much to learn

I don't dream of a perfect mosque, only
a few square inches of ground
that will welcome my forehead,
no questions asked

My little mosque is as decrepit
as my little heart. Its narrowness
is the narrowness in me. Its windows
are boarded up like the part of me that prays

I went to the mosque
when no one was there
No One was sweeping up
She said: This place is just a place
Light is everywhere. Go, live in it
The Mosque is under your feet,
wherever you walk each day

REFERENCES

Epigraphic Quranic translations, some of them amended by Mohja Kahf, based on the original Arabic and on Abdullah Yusuf Ali. *The Meaning of the Holy Qur'an*. Beltsville, MD: Amana, 2008.

Epigraph on page 000: *Sahih al-Bukhari, Arabic-English*. Translated by Muhammad Muhsin Khan. Beirut: Dar Al Arabia, 1985, 4: 376–77.

Epigraph on page 000: *Forty Hadith Qudsi of Imam al-Nawawi*. Translated by Ezzeddin Ibrahim. Chicago, IL: Kazi, 1998.

Epigraph by Meccan woman Um Ma'bad on page 000 translated by Mohja Kahf from: Ibn Taifur (Abi al-Fadl Ahmad bin Abi Taher). *Balaghat al-Nisa'*. Beirut: Dar al-Hadatha, 1987, 67.